JAMES RUSSELL
THE BROWN BREAD SONNETS

Newton-le-Willows

Published in the United Kingdom in 2025,
by The Knives Forks And Spoons Press,
51 Pipit Avenue,
Newton-le-Willows,
Merseyside,
WA12 9RG.

ISBN 978-1-916590-10-6

Copyright © James Russell 2025.

The right of James Russell to be identified as the author of this work has been asserted by them in accordance with the Copyrights, Designs and Patents Act of 1988. All rights reserved. No part of this publication may be reproduced, stored in a retrieval system, transmitted in any form or by any means, electronic, photocopying, recording or otherwise, without prior permission of the publisher.

Acknowledgements:

There are autobiographical elements in this, so my wife Carole bore some brunt. Thank goodness she was more patient and helpful than was Clovis's wife. I was very lucky. The book is dedicated to her.

For Carole

THE BROWN BREAD SONNETS

The Brown Bread Sonnets

1

'All dolled up to Dixie' is a phrase my mother
Used to use (why *Dixie?*) to mean anybody who'd made
An effort, perhaps too much of one. It need not
Have been a woman, and I'm extending it now to writing:
To this piece of writing. You see, this, as you can tell,
Is really prose. Though, the kind of prose that's
Gone on holiday (to scatter some Wittgenstein
Sparkle), because it has been hotelled into
Fourteen-line stanzas and given caps to the left
(Quick march!). It looks like sonnets if you half-
Close your eyes and care less. I will, though,
Avoid iambs, while, who knows, maybe veering
Near there as we reach the final two stanza lines
Where we may even stumble on some rhymes.

2

Stories go better in prose. Imagine a tale done
In the style of J. H. Prynne, and thread
These stars together. This story will be a thin,
Dark one, about Clovis L. Beecham. *Clovis?*
Who the hell names their offspring that? Nobody
In France is called Clovis. It's like naming your kid
Ethelred or Cnut. Blame his dad, a droll man
With a compliant wife. The couple had been to see
Chabrol's *Les Cousins*. No-one in it was called Clovis,
Though a seedy Chancer was nicknamed that. Dad was
The kind of man who'd call his son Crusher
Or Slippy or Dodger. Such a thought would
Evoke his smirking smile, broadening to a crack
When he considered that the 'L' stood for Leslie.

3

Truly his father's son, the world amused him
(Dangling modifier ahoy!) and gave him quiet scope
For mischief. He never worried, was ever cool.
At his elite school his nickname was Alf, after the
Mad-mag icon Alfred E. Newman. Indeed, his lazy
Grin was Newmanoid and he often tilted
His head in a quite dopey way: though he was very
Clever. Those who *liked* him called him Alf.
The rest called him Hovis, or Brown Bread,
Or Bread-Boy, or Browner (a buggery reference).
We pause. 'Brown bread' is rhyming slang for 'dead'.
We'll think about death through these cod sonnets —
The chances of an early bath. But there will be no gloom.
That scratching? Just death, the mouse in the room.

4

No gloom ever attached itself to Clovis. He was
A creature of light: his demeanour, his tastes,
His love of the richly windowed; it's his element —
Light. His progress up the world from nappies to
Education to employment was light-touch, effortless.
He breathed light in and out. I'll use the past tense,
Implying nothing by it, and pause again to say that
Throughout I'll be unspecific (just 'education' say),
Failing to scatter the mind-numbing particularity
That prose affords (for that very reason) and so
I can be airily allusive about all things medical.
To use detail here would be, well, *depressing*.
I know sad sacks who can rattle off their eleven
Prescription meds in four seconds and four syllables.

5

But ... at a party, moving away from Clovis
To talk to someone else was like leaving a cinema
On a sunny afternoon: their blinding intensity
Compared to him. You see, his lightness was of the
Light kind: a reassuring luminance, the intersect
Of no darkness and weightlessness. This makes him
Sound dully safe, a gravitas-free space. Not at all.
Back to dad. What the more intellectual son did with
Their shared temper was to bake it into love for
Surrealism. He'd written a book on the subject
Entitled *Rethinking Genetic Epistemology Even:
Real Surrealism*, whose mission was to 'kick out
All the bores, Breton, Bataille and the rest',
The theory-drunk pen-pushers farting in the nest.

6

For Clovis it was a simple thing: a clash of —
Don't say of semantic domains — of forms of
Life? (pasties and verb phrases; bowels and
Daisies) and when they clash something is released
Like sheer white light from a rock, overturning
The universal law of coherence to leave us free-standing
In a field of speaking heifers, a stretching of consciousness
Into the light of unreason. A far cry from the dark
Of the sub-mind and the maundering fantasy of half-
Science and half-hearted politics. Was he confusing
Surrealism with Dada? No: it's not about art. One
Who arranges a row of quinces beneath their flat-
Screen TV is a surrealist, as is one who wants to call
Their rugby team *The Thinking Trap* or *My Milk Book*.

7

Much of the book was dark, bristling with reasons why
The English do not excel at surrealism. Desmond
Morris's ('Desmong Moo-Cow's') 'babyish' paintings
And Poems, N.F. Simpson's ('N.F. Denis-Potter's')
'Laboured, airless' plays, these little old men who explain
That from the upper deck of the bus down from Acton to
Turnham Green there can be seen at a roundabout run-off
On a dressing table a photo of Queen Victoria between
Two cricket balls. And all of this must spur the question:
How did Clovis put food (or pine-needles? or breath?) on
The table? He was the most powerful arts
Administrator in the UK, a public figure. The book
turned up his quietly ambiguous persona to a din.
This Beecham, what is one supposed to make of him?

8

Of this tall angular man who dresses like a Lord
Who was, as someone said, the most clean-shaven
Man in London, who had millimetres of hair cropped
By *Trumpers* every ten days. No! (someone else said)
Not like a Lord, but like a President of France — a
Mitterrand, a Chirac, or especially a Giscard.
And like these he was married with ... mistresses.
He acted as if this were expected of him. He'd explained
To Susan when they met that this was the only kind
Of marriage he could contemplate. Meanwhile, he
Mimed a tennis shot saying 'The ball's in your court
Mademoiselle'. As his pluses outweighed this mad minus
She took him on (she was that kind of woman). They
Had two daughters and their life was calm-happy-strange.

9

He sometimes took his latest mistress to arts socials
Introducing her, perhaps, as 'my nieces's best friend's
Estate agent's landscape gardener' or 'my mistress',
Which folks often thought was a joke too. *They* were
Never jokes, often like deep friendships; they never
Overlapped and never really left his life. His life ...
As I say: strange. He was rich enough to live anywhere
In London, but lived in an unfashionable corner of west
West London in a rambling red-brick villa by a common
Shrouded in green — peaceful in a David Lynch way.
To him it was as open to the sky as Lincolnshire
(For Susan, as exciting). A journalist once called the road-
Racing cyclist Tommy Simpson's off track style 'sardonically'
Elegant. Clovis lived suburban life sardonically.

10

We darken now. Sardonic in speech too, he'd say:
"I've had surrealism thrust upon me, or Dada,
Or one of those adolescent sitcoms that scrapes laughs
From freeform smashing up. My job is to help to
Support the arts and my job is to strangle them
In their cradle, 'cus it's cheaper innit though butt."
All governments retained the strangle mandate;
And here was a man who loved all the arts and hated
Doing this bidding, till one day this happened. He'd
Had to announce that much of the National Theatre
Would have to move to Leicester ('cus it's cheaper innit
Though butt). He said he'd defend this on Radio 4 where a
Tigerish interviewer charged against an open door.
"A disgrace!" said Clovis to tiger red-faced on the floor.

11

"You didn't really expect me to DEFEND this
Did you? It's as if I've been crucified on one of
Gilbert and George's TURD CROSSES. If I climb down
The shit will stick to me. But I will. Are you
Following my line of thought, oh teenage daydream?
I'm resigning over this. It's shit too far. Toodle pip!"
He left the studio fragrantly. Many thought this
Was just a provocation; but it was *sous*-
Realism: the rock-bottom line. It sounded like
A jet of freezing anger, but it had been mulled
And cognized. Clovis had had enough. He did not
Need to work. Now he could *assimilate* the things
He'd failed to nurture. He would revert to his native
Self, taking extremest care never to be 'creative'.

12

I just about recall a routine Peter Cushing
Horror: a gentleman retires to a cottage to taste
The fruits. Roses round the door, lattice windows, wing-
Back chair, the needle dips to Sibelius, leather-
Bound poetry in hand, schooner of fine fino at
Elbow ... *Ahhh* ... cue the ghoul sneaking up behind —
Where my memory gives out. My point? Poor
Peter was already strapped to the turd cross before
The ghoul showed up. The hell of the passive, assim-
ilating as a patient of the world. Who wouldn't
Surreally yearn for the opposite life-form to shock
Action out of it. Everyone, especially Susan, knew
The withdrawal idea stank: exhibitions in the day,
Opera in the evening, the common, and nail filing?

13

This could not be *retirement:* too young; and looked it.
More to this than met the eye? No. Fact is, the plan
Never had time to die a natural death. Second fact is,
He hadn't been joking when he used to say, "Hobbies? Yes:
Drinkin', smokin', and sittin'. Why walk when God's
Given us taxis!" He looked fit, but wasn't. With a
Vital juice gone (don't say adrenalin) his body staged a
Counter-attack. Look, I can't bear to catalogue this now;
Must put it off. Body aside, this was a new Clovis,
This President of France as a punter who pleased
Himself. Though not Susan, despite his being happily
Mistress-less. He'd travel to Richmond or Tufnell
Park to have tea with an ex, which seemed pathetic
To her. Her husband should surprise, be energetic.

14

The body won't be denied. It speaks: "You opted
To be a non-agent, recipient, passive, well,
My friend, let's get physical. Now you can be a
Patient. See if you can get a laugh out of that."
Its first shot had come a while ago: pains like
Needles up his knees. He'd bought a snakewood cane
With a silver handle; that would not stop the pain.
Only replacement by titanium would do that, which
Happened to his left knee a year later and which
Changed him utterly. He was a laboratory frog
Spread for dissection. The right knee being done a year
Later hammered it home till he felt as if a giant syringe
Had been shoved into him and much of his essence
Drawn out. That would at least have been a simple tale.

15

How's this for nuance? Before his first knee job
They found some heart irregularity, and after the
Second his heart rate went bananas until he was
Given a modest beta blocker dose, which they
Later terminated. He didn't question it, as
They made him feel inert and dizzy. Drinking pink
Wine in this fools' paradise he fell into a wall
Having dropped awareness like a china cup.
"You turned white then red like a traffic light," said
Susan. The next few weeks were a tutorial
On the flimsiness of consciousness and the
Slipperiness of memory ... *I must hold on to this
Sliver of moth wing ... Did I see or imagine her
Do that?* He'd had enough. He called an ambulance.

16

Beneath the occasional bleep of a monitor
In A&E he felt relaxed. Each bleep meant his heart
Rate had touched 200 bpm, so this time the beta
Dose was an emphatic one. Inertly
Dizzy became the new black. You'd think these betas
Would help his blood pressure. Not so: it could go
Bananas too. But he decided he was med-
icated enough (plus blood thinners, four glaucoma eye-
drops a day), insisted he had White Coat Syndrome. 'Nope',
They said, and gave him two BP meds: one that made him itch
And one that made his ankles swell. Meanwhile, let's hear
It for his abdominal aortic aneurism,
Which only stopped growing when his ankles swelled.
As Lester Young sort of said, 'that was how the bread smelled'.

17

Let's hear it for his hernia! He spent as much
Mind energy pondering what made it pop out or not
As he used to spent outwitting the Treasury.
Let's not forget his twice-daily asthma inhaler, his
Hearing aids (often blocked with wax); but above all
Let's hear it for The Big Issue: "You need a cataract
Op," twice refused due to high BP. "Shall we try again?" —
"No lets give up," his darker self replied. "I'd rather be
Half-blind and deaf than be mucked about by you." —
"Why don't you tell the surgery about your hernia?"
Susan said. — "It's handy. I hook my sweatpants to it
To hold them up." This was the only kind of joke he made
The real joke being that he would ever wear sweatpants.
She quietly said one day: "It's as if you've killed yourself."

18

This is in a hole and I'm gonna keep digging.
I hope to build on the bedrock (*bless!*). Cardiology
Had said coffee is out (he loved it) and only a
Little tea. A teeny bit of booze is alright: *Impossible*
For him, so he gave all up. A dizzy stroll round
The common on clog-like feet with the prospect of
Mint tea in the evening. Susan as a prospect?
Even when a mistress was at her height, he would,
To use Chuck Berry's phrase, keep the home fires
Burning. But now the fire was beneath a concrete
Bushel. OK, stand back! We're about to strike bedrock.
One day he went to an exhibition of late Raphael
At the National, returning to spit contempt
For those attending, not a single word about the art.

19

Meanwhile, he coughed compulsively — accusing her
Of giving him a cold. She turned away, then back,
Said: "I'm off. I want to live in *London* not in this
Nicely-nicely non-place. I could bear it when Clovis
Was here, but he's replaced by this moaning minus.
I've found a little terrace in Kentish Town." — "I'll give
You the money," — "No you won't." And that was it.
It all happened so quickly, sound-tracked by his
Ghoulish cough. Here's bedrock now. Not a nice
Place to be: grey sky above, nowhere to
pitch a tent. And marbled into the bedrock
We find Clovis with a back ache, a hip ache and
A knee ache, turning day by day into unbearable
Pain. He necked codeine, all in Sue's ignorant absence.

20

She mustn't see the full extent, must not know.
She'd come, minister to him effectively, then ... go.
He had no choice but to settle into bedrock life:
Walking with sticks, constant pain, dreading a cough,
Unable to ... lets just say, in John Mortimer's phrase,
(Re Coleridge) he was a 'stranger to the lavatory',
But an intimate of each laxative variety.
He met those snakes-and ladders complications, though
Life was simple, like fighting a war is simple.
Eventually (a socialist, so he stuck with the
NHS), an MRI said he had a crushed vertebra.
"You're a lucky man," said a small black-clad man,
"The bone stayed clear of the descending nerve bundle." —
"And you're a fucking *Advanced Clinical Practitioner*."

21

Of course, he didn't say that. These days his tongue was
Bitten to distraction. It was bitten harder
When his loyal, but bossy, daughter May was there
To help him do the basics, to cook, bringing it home
To him how sharp and coarse his tongue had been with Sue.
He knew that over the past few months he'd been
Pouring black ink over their love letters. This bog-stranger
Didn't like to eat, and took on the aspect of
A vindictive cadaver. Friends would call round
And would feel unwelcome till he skilfully poured
Wine over their discomfort, biting still harder
Into his tongue, ravening to unravel each
Grim fact about his bodily story, wanting to say:
"It's as if my worst enemy has come to stay."

James Russell

22

Each time I slip into tee-tum tee-tum and rhyme
I feel farther from the truth, at least the following
Kind of truth. It seemed as if (too much as-iffing?)
He was his body's ally willy nilly. He
Was fighting on his body's side, and this made him
Mindless, a creature whose emotions were thing-
Processes, who could not think as he used to do.
For instance, an old friend had once turned up at one
Of the parties he and Sue used to give with a new
Girlfriend, very young, very sexy, in a short leather
Skirt. "Tell me Pete," he'd said, when the young lady had
Excused herself, "does she take philosophical points?"
No, Peter Peacocke wasn't a philosopher.
And if he had been it would have ruined the remark.

23

Clovis never gave the mind-body relationship
A second's thought, but if he had it would be as
Two surreally clashing life-forms. So here he was
Behind his body yearning for mentality
Across the great divide, telling taxi drivers
Just how bits of him were impaired. "You sound different,"
Sue would say in their rare phone calls, "calmer, self-
Contained" which he translated as 'spiritually
Dead'. But he still had his thinking parts and using
These he couldn't miss the blinding question: Why should
Coughing, however violent, fracture a vertebra?
A rib maybe, but vertebra L3? There were
Umpteen blood tests, pee investigations, dark
Mentions of darker nasties. This was now his ball park.

24

Osteoporosis, bone-marrow cancer: these
Weren't a few of his favourite things, but somehow
They failed to rise above his horizon by virtue
Of the dream-like way he'd come to think his
Solitary thoughts. Such nasties were of the body
And so magically divorced from him *qua* him.
Though his thinking parts darkly knew the captain
Goes down with his ship: his body must not fail.
Meanwhile, in his cabin he burnished his laxative
Connoisseurship, watched *Pointless* on the TV,
Read Zola to meet healthy people worse off than
He was. His snakewood cane was too elegant
For what he had in body. It was a peasant stick that
Steadied him down his corridors, happy as a brick.

25

The stick steadied him into cabs that only
Ended at hospitals or surgeries, where he gathered
Facts: he'd lost two stone in weight and two inches in height;
He saw how crushed L3 had bullied the flow (where does
It go?) of cerebrospinal fluid, stopping just short
Of nerves; he learned it would be a long wait for the
Bone-density scan results and the blood-n-pee
Ones. But things were getting better: the weather,
His eating, his walking, the pain. Yes, *things:* physicals
Scored up to his enemy-host. His spirit was
Enjoying the glorious emptiness of no
Medical words. No injunctions, there'd been, for weeks.
Then the phone rang with the waited-for feared answer:
Blood-pee proteins consistent with bone-marrow cancer.

26

The doc had started in his eager-beaver pretend
High voice, rattling through the many all-clears
Then dipping like a disappointed headmaster's.
Then more lightness-spin saying it could "easily be
No more than an infection. And the 'good news'
(At this point 'You have a week to live' would have filled
That bill) is that we have a date in July for a
Bone biopsy at Charing Cross." After the call, Clovis
Had a sudden onrush of giddy goat
Singing *My Myeloma* to the tune of that phoney
Knack hit *My Sharona*. He could not stop mouthing
The guitar riff. He couldn't start the process of knowing
That it could kill him in five years. Myeloma means bone-
Marrow cancer like 'beanz meanz farts'. But soon he knew.

27

Myeloma would explain at a stroke both the crushed
L3 and the delinquent white blood cells' proteins.
"Itsh the mosht parsimonioush hypothesish,"
He lisped in vicious and pointless satire to himself
On his now regular hobbles on the Common.
And he was *absurdly* thin. He had been back
Gluttonising normally for weeks now, but in his
Trilby he reminded himself of Bill Burroughs after
An all-water diet. The chance of prematurely
Ceasing to exist was sickly liberating. It was
'As if some pressing but vaguely understood oblig-
ation had suddenly been lifted from [his] shoulders,
That some final examination for which [he] could
Never have been properly prepared had been cancelled'.

28

It's not important who I'm quoting here. It doesn't
Matter, not even to me. And this slight assault
On the logic of his position can only evoke
His mood. It was a partly-destructive mood
(If a 10-year-old boy is asked what he'd do on
His last day on earth there would probably be much
smashing up and charging into girls' changing rooms).
But benign too. It opening him up, opened him
To people immediate to him. They didn't know
Him nor he them. For the first time — 'vaguely under-
stood obligation' gone to be himself — he chatted.
He hobbled long-distance to a dreary 'Avenue'
To a newsagent, he'd once bonded with over his view
Of Wes Streeting ('arsehole, needs kicking in the balls').

29

This wasn't typical of Tas (his name). He was
The all-accepting, ever-amused Smile behind
The counter, something between a therapist and a
Chat-show host. He had the knack of taking
A conversational gambit and elevating it
Like a Frisbee or flying saucer, brightening
The whatever for just long enough. He was, though, an
Eccentrically thoughtful socialist and strong
Despiser of bullshit. This was *all* one knew of him.
One day Clovis was a little late and all the
Guardians had gone, "Never mind. Now I'll put one back for you.
What's your name?" — "Mick Avory," he shot back, surprising
Himself. — "OK, Mick. How's about an unused *Telegraph?*"
As part of their routine they shared a belly laugh.

30

He'd joined a club. Let's call them *The Morning Men*:
Nothing like Powell's *Afternoon Men*: elderly open
Systems, rendered innocuous by age, affable.
Francis Bacon said of being offered a knighthood
'Terribly ageing'. Yes, the whippersnapper Clovis
Might have been aged by this had he followed their lead
And stood to the left of the counter, having collected
Their paper, and shot the breeze with the professional Tas.
One long, snow-white twig in red cagoule and Covid
Mask even laughed at Tas's 'Good morning's'.
No, he was in and out for a homeopathic dose.
Like a Twitter twat, he'd perfected the reducing
Of sentences to fit the slim interstices
Between the visits of the hard-core members.

31

"You're shrinking and not just physically," Susan
Said in one of their rare Zoomings in. Meaning,
In her skeletal academic way, that his concerns
Were now micro: local WhatsApp group small, football small.
His bullshit freedom was a kind of freedom to
Ignore the looming monsters and scan ripples and
Cuticles. And, yes, they were Tas-small too. So much of him
Wondered how things stood in his shop in the afternoon.
Was he grave with sour old ladies, having handed
Them their *Mails* and *Expresses*? He knew what he would do.
He'd hobble out there at 1PM, lunch at a
Passable-looking café called *The Butterfly Ball*,
Then he would (fielding all the pizzazz he could employ)
Pop in for a birthday card for his other daughter Joy.

32

After a *croque monsieur* with gratis boiled kale
He pizzazzed across the road to see Tas engaged
With what sounded like a girl probably buying sweets
(The card island occluded some of Tas and all of her).
Tas seemed amused by her. She trilled. He casualled
"Just looking for a birthday card for my daughter Joy." —
"OK mate." *Mate!* He was right: it's the female turn
In the afternoon. But kids! Then he heard her say *'Ciao.'*
Do kids say *Ciao?* And then he got the shock of his life.
She was perfection: about 50; a helmet-bob
Of blonde hair; a strange-chic outfit, like a bellboy's; and
To crown her, a light-grey beret; under which
Piercing blue eyes and a lip-tight grin that could only
Be called 'cheeky'. Face it: only be called 'sexy'.

33

He quickly chose any card. Joy wouldn't notice
(She was not bossy, but she was solipsistic).
"She's a piece of work," said Tas very coolly. —
"How do you mean?" No reply. — "Is she regular?" —
"Dunno. Why don't you ask her?" Then more Tas
Laughter, but not quite of the sweet-meat morning kind.
On her way out she'd touched his arm saying in that
10-year-oldly brazen voice: "What a lovely old name:
Joy. I wish you much of it, er, *Card*ew." Clovis
Did not know or care what day it was. He wanted
To hail a cab and follow her. "Tell you what Tas.
I had lunch at the *Butterfly* caff and think
I'd like to repeat the experience." — "Begorrah!" —
"So sometimes I'll call in for my paper around now,"

34

"Kale Kale Kale Kale Kale Kale Kale Kale Kale Kale,"
Intoned Tas to the tune of the Python Spam Song.
"I'll have chicken wrap, kale, coleslaw, kale, pasteis
De nata, and double kale. Never say hold the kale!"
This was a new Tas, who seemed let down by Clovis.
Would take a blind man not to see what Clovis was about.
There followed ten days in which the ripple minutiae
That decorated his bullshit freedom from gravity
Was ripped from him. First he returned to The Morning Men,
But Tas had changed. Not even Wes Streeting trash talk
Could stir him. Then to *Butterfly* lunches, plus *post hocs*.
Wandering over for batteries or stamps or ... he flagged.
No sign. Finally, to a lonely toastie — kale-smeared:
He chewed, simpered innerly; and she appeared.

35

Their eyes, smiles, and words met and resolved into
Sharing a table. He abandoned his green-stained toastie
And began lunch again. His fear had been that she
Would turn out to be thick. She wasn't that.
She knew very little, but she was almost scarily
Fast-perceiving and shrewd. So her face told the truth
(Though you would not associate 'truth' with it).
Her speech evoked Daisy Ashford, and he felt
That if it were transcribed it would be mis-spelt.
He heard the impishness, mixed with sly cruelty that
Her smile promised. "You seem too young," she said, "to be
A moth about The Man in the Moon." Tas was not
An obvious moon man, but this somehow hit the target.
"Get close, Cardew," she sparkled, "to see his craters?"

36

The sudden tetch-whip cracked: "Not Cardew, please! Start
Calling me Clovis." — "*Clovis*. You mean your name's actually
Clovis? Like the alcoholic brother of someone
On the Simpsons?" He stonewalled and she got the message.
The conversation settled as she skilfully drew out
His bio (she had never heard of the Arts Council).
And then his health ... "I refuse to call them issues."
Her grin was gone and her eyes sparkled only to the
Butterfly cruet. She gave a plaintive, ancient
Look. He finished and she laid a hand over his.
If she says, 'Oh you poor lamb', he thought, I leave.
"There are so many things that could be said and all fail.
Just know that I feel for you, as I know how it feels.
Lets talk more and often. Let's try private meals."

37

Too heavy on the fennel seeds, on the sausage meat, on
The tomato purée above all. But what he'd
'Rustled up' paled beside the point inside his quietly
Splendid house. She drank with care; he vicariously.
They were too heavy on the small talk. Then it was
Like ten minutes to go in a goalless draw: too
Heavy on the heaviness. They were somehow
Paralyzed by their being there together at all.
Evening sun on glutinous pasta. So much
Unsaid. Her grin took a quick turn to a purpose.
"I have something to say Clovis and I think it has
To be said, especially by me. Over two years ago —
It was a corny winter's day — I was told that I had
Four months to live. I said that's not good. It's very bad.

James Russell

38

But here I am a living breathing nay hyperven-
tilating girl who can dance and pivot and recite.
They examine me ... and I pass all the MOTs. This
Means something gigantic for you Clovis. It will
knock your socks off." — "What ... [Till this point he'd
Buried biopsy fears; and now he was beside
Them in their cave] *does* it mean for me?" — "It's obvious.
But you know nothing about me, so here's the tour ... "
It wasn't riveting, though watching her speaking was.
Father in the RAF, unsettled life, leaving
'Uni' early, drifting, bad marriage, bought a hand-made
Jewellery business with divorce money, went bust in
The Covid time, presently 'experimenting.' Nothing
To engage the teeth, which longed for a chewy something.

39

The evening didn't end as he'd hoped it would.
He called her a cab from the firm with which [*dig the
Poetry!*] he had an account, at once writing down
Her address before it left his mind. So much was
Coming and going from it since they'd met. She could
Write anything on his blank slate, for she'd enchanted
Him as a woodland spirit might. Her face — pixie face —
Should really be coming into focus in the centre
Of a flower in the kind of Buñuel film he loved.
These dinners continued chez him as she drip-fed
Droplets about her tale of miracle recovery.
The old Clovis would have cold-shouldered it, but this
Silly-potent tale seeped in, you know, below the belt.
On which: they were starting to kiss hard at evening's end.

40

"Just give me time," she'd whimper. — "I s-suppose so," he gulped.
He'd replay, in the daytime, her talking Buñuel head:
"Everybody knows that the placebo effect works."
His memory speaks. "Well all one does is to *harness* it
When talking to oneself and say, say, 'Tumour go away'." —
"But how do you say it and believe it? You can tell me
'Now there you have me'." She took his laughter sportingly.
But one day she did not. She had been trying to get her
Meaning across. He lightly teased. She bitterly cried,
Rallied, kissed him deeply and they went straight to bed.
This changed everything utterly. *In part*, the fact of
His fragile painful, constraining spine, was the wand, whose
Presence wrought magic. She said: "Now d'you like my meaning?"
By the way, her name was Penelope Greening.

41

He'd crossed the river and now he was on her side.
Little question that she had not crossed to him.
Who cares? Not him: he levitated in their afterglows.
In one, she: "What are you thinking?" — He: "That placing chips
Under those ugly heating lights dries them out and
Makes them rubbery" (she'd have to get used to this). —
"And you?" — "To tell you that two years ago I also
Threw away all my medications, and have never felt
More fine." — "No, what I should have been thinking is that
I must do this myself." She looked shocked, almost scared.
"But really you trust me that far! Your blood pressure, heart,
Glaucoma, and the rest? For all you know I could be
Playing you like a yo-yo. I could be a Maid Marian
Impersonator." — "Or a perfectly proportioned sprite."

42

He didn't tell her that his will to do this predated
[*Dig the poetry!*] their meeting, and deflected her with
"Did someone once pass some arcane knowledge onto you?" —
"Oh yes!" Her eyes blazed. "They'd kindly given me my
Death sentence in the February and it was mid May.
I'd calculated I had a week or so to go
So I went on holiday to the Isle of Wight.
One day I was picking wild flowers. Didn't know their names
But I think I called one Lilly of the Valley.
With my lovely varied bunch I made my way back
To the cottage I'd rented, till I got lost, quite lost
And I was in pain — my poor belly as usual.
I was at the end of a narrow lane at whose other
End I knew, just knew, was a big fine stuccoed house.

43

Standing there, stock still like in the first scene of a play,
Were a horse and its minder. The horse looked sort-of
Human, as a police chief might in his best uniform
To face the press with sheen; but with coloured ribbons all
Flowing round it: not rosettes, random ribbons. And the man
Was very tall and handsome all in green in snooker
Table cloth togs. I had to walk right in front of them but
As I did a pain shot into my tummy as if
I had been stabbed. I *had* to grab myself and dropped
My flowers in the dirt. The man struggled to help
Me pick them up and hold the bridle at the same time.
'What happened?' he said in and old-style BBC
Voice. I explained about my growth and he looked long
At me. His face was perfect but also pretty wrong.

44

I mean he had this thick thick manly beard but his skin
Was that of a lady model, a creamy pure,
And his eyes looked made up. I longed to pull his beard
To see if it stood true. He spoke: 'If you have the spirit,
And not everybody has the spirit, you can speak
Direct and clear to your malady and tell it to depart.
The battle between spirit and matter is never over
And there are no victors; but some have access to ... '
Just then a gust of wind blew ribbons into
The horse's eyes making it rear, so I made myself
Absent. Back at the cottage I arranged the flowers
In a vase and doing so felt a sudden strength
Like that gust of wind, but a permanent gust.
'Go away rotten growth', I said. 'Go you must'."

45

While Penelope was speaking he was gazing at her
Naked breasts as if expecting them to pipe up
Like a Greek chorus. Nothing would surprise him now
Because he'd taken a holiday from disbelief.
He swam in belief as he used to do when acting
In a play in his student days. But, yes, the first
Thing that he did when she'd gone home was to gather all
His meds and flush them down the bog, except the eye-drop
Efforts and inhalers which ... [*who cares!*]. A little later
He was swept up by his own and explicable
Gust of power: health power. The pink of his eye-
Whites cleared to pure white (no blood thinners). No
Nightly itching, so no self-smearing with *Eurax* cream
(No BP med). Was he living or dying the dream?

46

Well, that's an essay question we can park. Meanwhile,
His ankle bones hove into modest view — especially
In the morning (no BP med again). Sudden head turns
Did not disorientate (no betas), while that indef-
inable grey stasis that had settled on him was gone
(No betas). When he tried a coffee and a glass
Of wine it felt like an assault. OK, but in
Declining them he was a victorious general
Palming away an offer in the best brothel
Of the conquered city (well maybe not that). Within
The limits of his hobble he could almost swagger.
But one day after a stronger than usual cup of tea
There was a palpitation that skewered him to his chair;
That made him feel spotlighted alone on a gusting heath.

47

It settled down and he sort-of did too, but it was
The 'alone' element that prickled him. Were they not
Partnered on this project? Yet here they were pacing
Themselves by spacing their meetings to avoid
The 'Passionate Intensity Thing' (to blend Yeats and Bush
Senior). He would go to see her, quite out of the blue.
Was this the beta-blocker lack talking back? Could be.
But the Passionate Intensity Thing meant that
Nothing could stall him. He knew the region where she lived:
In one of the mediocre streets around
That shed-like Waitrose he sometimes visited.
He sang to himself *On the street where you live* as
He flipped away bin-day debris with his stick.
Cement gardens, fucked up gates, more dead than quick.

48

"Oh! I was expecting Penelope." — "She's in.
She expecting you?" — "No but ... " — "Wass your name?" — "Clovis" —
"Oh, yeah, right. Hang about." He shouts indoors "Peee, Peee!
Clovis is here to see you. All clear water, or what?
Come in Clo mate." The young man was what Clovis called
A cartoon: his features too unambiguous, upfront.
His absurdly neat beard seemed to have been made
From the same black Velcro-like stuff as his hair.
He was lucidly handsome, but in a way that such
A one would have been drawn on her beloved *The Simpsons*.
She then appeared in tired blue jeans that scraped the floor,
unmade-up, and with a spray of rattiness. Cool.
"Vaughan, this is Clovis and Clovis this is my *lodger*,
Vaughan." Vaughan was amused. Clovis fumed in a genteel way.

49

No need to report the awkward shuffling of what
Was said before they ended up together in the front room,
Or reflect on Vaughan's "Why don't you two pop into the front
Room and I'll make myself scarce?" She wasn't pleased to see
Him. But once they'd kissed and settled on the drab settee
He'd ceased to regret coming. "I'm not taking to
Your lodger." — "He can be a bit pushy, Vaughan." — "And thick." —
"He's a web designer." — *"Ja und?"* — "Eh?" — "I've missed you." —
"Good. Are you alright?" He told her about the post palpit-
ation panic, and she smiled out this: "Go forward. You can't
Look back and be turned into a pillar of salt like Lot." —
"It was Lot's wife [ignored]. In any case that is quite
Beside the point. I thought we'd formed a unity
But right now, I mean now, I am the only unity."

James Russell

50

A hurt or angry silence from her, while he needed
A pee [*Dig the poetry!*]. "Is the loo upstairs?"
Suddenly she was tender: "The stairs are awkward."
They were: the handrail was on the left so he had to
Hand himself up on the right, on the stairs *themselves*.
He was glad she did not witness his hateful grovel.
Vaughan did, standing at the stair-top looking down
Smiling his David Beckham smile: "Going great guns Clo.
Much impressed. Plenty of originality there."
Clovis froze, looked up, hissed through his teeth: "Hold your tongue."
Vaughan vanished. On his way back from the loo was visible
Vaughan in a computery room typing at cartoon speed.
As soon as he'd returned to her, still in her tender state,
Vaughan 'popped in' offering tea and the words: "No hard feelings mate."

51

Something between them had been repaired in the sense
Of 'patched up'. They were holding hands like teenagers
When Vaughan 'popped in' like mother to ask her if it was
Blue or Black bin day next week. His glassy eyes
Photographed them. "If it's too much, darling, go back on the
Medications." — "No, I'm committed now. It's the right course." —
"You hate any kind of constraint, don't you sweetheart?"
He knew this showed incredible insight: it lay
At the heart of his love of surrealism. Their
Parting was warm, but ambiguous. They would lunch
Next day at *Butterfly*. He stepped from the house into
The muggy day and into that feeling all lovers know:
Where a sudden fragile darkness kills the spring,
Which only makes the need a more desperate thing.

52

He'd had a too-long walk to and from the bus-stops,
So at home he hobbled about a bad-pain day.
How *could* she share a house with that semi-human!
Nothing, rhymed, added up, or chimed today. Freedom
From medical rules meant he could eat a hot (betas)
Curry tonight. He enjoyed it little and longed for
Tomorrow's lunch. Approaching *Butterfly* he quietly
Decided to avoid their skimmed-milk tea, when the first thing
He saw was Vaughan at a window-seat waving ...
"A million apols from P, but ... " and he was off in
His London drawl. He recited with verve
The lie: "Like P agreed at the last mo to be
Keynote speaker at a workshop on faith healing
At a academic conference in uh in uh Ealing."

53

The girls had been forever 'chucking' boyfriends by text.
He was forever telling them how 'disgusting' this was.
Well, she deserved disgusting — a beautiful fit.
"Hello, Vaughan lied to me yesterday. He said he was
Named after Ralph Vaughan-Williams and I said LIAR.
Then he said 'No Clo it was Winford Vaughan-Thomas'
LIAR. Then he admitted it was Frankie Vaughan.
Now kindly fuck off out of my life for good. CLB."
But the no-meds project would continue.
He got out-of-breath more easily climbing stairs;
There were times he felt he had to take a deep
Breath because heart-beats faltered; but he was *fresher*.
A reason just beneath thought that was cloudy but strong:
Van Morrison's words, he'd *get down to what is really wrong*.

54

Or maybe it was like stripping off a bandage to
Reveal a wound which then might heal? Or maybe I
Hear votes for 'like sparklingly foolhardy bullshit'?
Would 5mg of beta blocker per day have
Settled his anger at her, at himself? I think not.
But through its mist he missed the Brigadoon of her.
Even the weather joined in — a spiteful summer rain.
He was supposed not to sit in an easy chair for more
Than half an hour at a time; but since her he had
Taken up old films as a hobby, especially
Late at night — the rebel because he had no cause.
Was that a backfiring car spotting the words of a young
Lana Turner? It was the knocker on a filthy night.
And there she stood, her beret and her hair were one.

55

"Can ... can I come in for five minutes, or stop here?"
Inside he offered her a towel, hairdryer, whiskey
And a stony face against any excuses for her not
Being at *Butterfly*. "No point in telling you,"
She said in a matronly voice, "why I sent Vaughan
Instead. That's a tiny thing compared to what I
Have to say. Clovis, Vaughan and I are crooks. He is a
Cyber criminal and I target men to get
Money out of them — old men, vulnerable men, and
Interested ones. If they're married there may well be
Blackmail too. I work up a kind of dependency
Then lie ('mummy needs an expensive operation'),
Or gently suggest they take out a standing order
For me. Could be legal, illegal, or on the border.

56

You must hate me." — "A little, but at least we're
Getting down to what is really wrong." — "Eh?" — "That stuff
About your fatal illness and the green man with the
Ribbony horse: all lies I assume." — "NO!" This was
Fiercely guttural. "What I came to say ... It's our bond
It's the road to my falling in love with you, and NOW
I'm in love with you, how can I be the crook to you?
That life is over. I told Vaughan we're finished." — "You mean?" —
"Yes, I've moved out, stayed last night in a nasty hotel." —
"I'll call a cab ... " — "Oh!" — "So you can get your stuff
And bring it here." — She drank her whiskey in one.
He felt he didn't love her, but he was in her train.
"I think of you and know that I was never in love before,"
She breathed. "You saved me. I can save you and set you free."

57

Part of him wanted to dive back into the world
Of Lana Turner, and part burned to celebrate and
Affirm. This last popped out like his hernia when
She was away collecting two enormous suitcases:
They should take something like a holiday, be absent
From London and the little world of Tas and *Butterfly*.
His impairment had shrunk him away from big London;
But there was an elsewhere. Let her chose where. She was
All for it, but wiped out. A further weaker whiskey
And she was asleep on the sofa. He left her.
Asleep she looked as young as her voice. Would Vaughan 'pop'
Round now for a cup of sugar? Had she done something
To his phone surreptitiously to feed a data lie
To the cyber criminal mastermind or 'mas-mi'?

James Russell

58

That evening, the real had become as brittle
As his bones. Given a crush or snap, anything
Could happen. He went sea-sick to bed and left
Her snoring. The next day had hard sun and tensile strength.
Though the question of where they would go drove a balsa
Wood car. "Sidmouth! You want to go to Sidmouth? Not
San Sebastian or a Greek island?" She said it — or
Rather nearby Ladram Bay — had mental ties to the
Time before, in her words, she 'took the crook route.'
"I know John Betjeman rates it, but for me
It's Sid-Nice-But-Dim." At which she spent rapturous
Minutes trying to describe the colour of what she
Called the cakey cliffs: "Between rotten strawberries
And milk chocolate, bicycle inner tubes that crumble."

59

In almost a bubble of happy, here he was
In the back of a hired Mercedes cuddling Penelope
Heading southwest in the sun, he knew this was
Unintelligent. But ... though but ... maybe but ... hold on.
Intelligence, he mused, is the enemy of art
And art and life are fused. His mind sped with the car.
Those Yankee novels ruined by higher education,
Thought-frozen music and artworks. Crack open the raw feels
And say Hello to the genie! He knew this was only
A project with built-in obsolescence; but ... though but ...
Maybe but ... hold on: let the present sun be whatever
Wallace Stevens meant by 'the sun.' Already here? Really?
Sidmouth front looked fresh, innocent, healthy. "Are you sure
This is the place Sir?" They'd pulled up outside mediocrity.

60

It was a red-brick, side-street guest house, well away
From the white or pink stuccoed glories that faced up
To the sea; *Seaborn* (sic) its name. Penelope
Had said it was 'brilliant' and 'homely' (easy to
Believe). It was 'run by friends of friends.' 'My friend's
Friend is my enemy,' he had said. 'Eh?' she
Had said. "Hi Penny," the mousey owner said, "and you
Must be ... ?" — "Clovey," he said, deciding to give it all
A run for its money. It was OK: chintzy, smelling
Of lavender with undernotes of *Benson and Hedges*.
They found a superb fish restaurant near the promenade.
He braved a glass of Chablis, which loosened his tongue.
Everything was loosened. They didn't speak much, and that night
Their love-making put it all in place and everything right.

61

Memories of the night sustained him through the fullest
Full English he had ever seen (fried bread, black pudding
And all) and just about sustained him through Penelope's
Plaints about how 'sad' it was they couldn't take the cliff path
Walk to Ladram Bay: "I mean your being stick-bound and all."
They sat on a bench on the front in the blazing sun
As she cast her eyes to the right towards the path leading
To the Ladram Shangri-La. "OK, my walking's pretty good
Right now. Let's at least struggle up the first stretch of
The path, then sit and gaze out to sea like geriatrics."
She kissed him. "Fancy a job as a carer now you're
Not a crook any more?" he said as she handed and yanked
Him to the top. "My crook career was a rehearsal
For that." This he ignored because the view was heavenly.

62

Restless, she wanted to press on, but there was no way
He would. He almost stood over a couple sitting
On a tree stump in the fulfilled hope his stick would persuade
Them away. They sat before a sky in what he called
'Heaven blue' that sat above an ultramarine sea
Sparkling with life. But the true heaven was the presence
Of three white-sailed yachts making their gentle way past.
He felt a peace he'd never known before. The yachts'
Movement was a resignation that spoke to him.
Bizarrely, this evoked not great poetry or music
But a fragment of Lou Reed's *Heroin*, about being
Born a thousand years ago and wearing a sailors suit
And hat and going from this land on to that. So was it
Just the chemical peace of numbness? No, no, no.

63

He looked at her in search of an echo, to find
A business-like blank. "Penny for 'em?" she said. "Hard to
Believe, but this fantastic view made me think of some lines
From *Heroin*." — *"I'm closing in on death?"* was her charmless thought.
At once she fired into life and waved joyfully
At something towards the town. What he saw cresting
The path was Vaughan — let it sink in — Vaughan, wearing
This season's trend of mini-shorts, and grinning fit to crack.
"Howdie doodie! I'm doing the trek to Lad Bay. Catch you
Later guys, maybe." He breathed deep and said "Does Vaughan
Shave his legs?" — "Oh yes," she glowed. "He's a cyclist — member
Of the West London Road Rac ... " — "Be QUIET." Later
After absolute silence she said he'd texted her to ask
"Me how I was and I let slip ... " Well, now he had a task.

64

He must choose kiss or kill. Right now he'd like to hire
A helicopter and drop her into 'Lad Bay,' then leave.
Her face crumpled into tears. "I've messed up big time."
The 'big time' spoiled it; but his heart softened.
They struggled through an awkward morning both trying
To say the right thing. They must have looked an earnest
Pair among the smiling families and wholesome fun.
After a cosy lunch she said she needed a nap [*dig*
The poetry!] so she slept as he read; then he crept out.
Figuring a bitter shandy wouldn't kill him, he went
Into a pub and ordered at the bar. A clap
On his back. "Lemme get you a proper drink Clo." —
"Why?" No, he decided he'd interrogate the sod.
"Doing the stick walk must put a strain on the old bod."

65

If truth could be squeezed through his gleaming chicklet teeth,
This was it. She had texted him to ask the number
Of his auntie [*dig* ...] as his auntie was the mouse
Who ran the guest house. He was 'staying with a mate.'
He liked 'to keep an eye on her.' "But you've split up!" —
"You could say that Clo. Yes, she had been given a
Terminal diagnosis, but the girl exaggerates.
She needs stability in her life. My advice
Is to give it to her Clo." His teeth were unstained
By lies; and Clovis believed him. "Are you
A cyber criminal?" — "Lol," he said, "L-O-L! I'm a
Bit-coin trader. Up and down mate. Up and down."
When he got back she was awake, troubled, and bug-eyed.
She writhed, said she felt sick; but his heart stayed inside.

66

This heart told him she was shamming, that she wanted
To get back to London, that she was bored. But he couldn't
Believe it. This was a new her: dignified and tacit, with
Absolute focus on her pain. She'd hold her right side.
"Can you phone your car people. I need to get to The
London Clinic." — "The London Clinic! You can aff ... " — "I'll tell
You later." In the car he was cruel enough
To question her, despite her state. Vaughan's auntie? —
"Didn't want to upset you." — The bit-coin business? —
"You think all they do is *legal?*" — Exaggerating? —
"I did not exaggerate that, nor the ribbon-horse story.
Now please *have a heart*. There's been a shift. I mean
My spirit is weakening: it's as if I can't catch my breath.
I need you to cuddle me up because I'm losing faith."

67

As he saw her disappear with the smaller of her two
Huge suitcases into the hotel-like building, seeing
Not frailty but alone-ness, he half-knew what she'd meant.
The least he could do was to surround her with his arms —
Which was a kind of clinging. Silence then from her
And the occasional gnomic text — how he hated
Fucking texts! — some of which said things like 'Docs say
Its really not to bad (*sic*)' or 'All these blinking tests.' 'Thinking
Of you' was the warmest they got, apart from the crosses.
But maybe he was too much of a 'word child', drawing
Sustenance from ... This thought was aborted in his kitchen
As he stood dreaming before his wall calendar.
Tomorrow was the day of his bone biopsy. Guilt
And duty and a kind of FOMO — all felt.

68

The medical world was winning; the material world
Was winning. "The results will be with your GP"
The Registrar said, "in a couple of days, but as
Important: your blood pressure is sky high, so I advise
An urgent visit to A&E." Of course he
Didn't do that and, I suppose, *of course* he ordered
A new prescription and doubled up his BP doses.
It was like a first day back at school. "Oh hell,
Where am I now!" He was booking an examination
For his hernia. There had been a cancellation so
It was soon. "Now that's a beauty," his favourite
Doctor said. "And another bit of beauty is that
Your biopsy was all clear, so we can lift up our hearts!"
Joyful he felt, but so much less than the sum of his parts.

69

He was off the hook — and back on another hook; but the
First fact flooded into him and buoyed him up. Oh dear,
Clovis was thinking in clichés ('parts', 'hook' and the rest)
To shield himself from the open field of choices
That crowded round him like ... like ... like ... what? cows? ravers?
The fact is he was not entirely relieved not to
Have [*dig it: the poesy*] a shortened life. He'd done enough
And felt a profound exhaustion surrounded by things
And projects he'd exhausted. He texted Penelope
To tell her the news. 'That's FAB. I'm fab too and docs
Say I can go home soon. Come and see me!!!!!! XXXXXX'
When he got to the room she'd told him there was (yup!) Vaughan
Stretched along her bed in shorts, his hands behind his head.
"Watcher Clo. Sad news mate: P's what they call brown bread."

70

"You mean?" — "Yeah, she's snuffed it." — "Why are you on her bed?" —
"I paid for the fucker." For the first time, Vaughan
Showed anger. "Not every day you lose your wife, Clo."
"*Wife?*" — "Yeah." — "She'd told me she was getting better and now
She's ... " — "P was not the most truthful bunny in the uh ... uh ... " —
"In the horse box? In the Waitrose queue? The most truthful
Spatula in the catacombs? The most truthful
Suppository in the jelly mould? The most truthful
Leaf blower in the final examiners' meeting?
The most truthful tear in the cheek lesion?
The most truthful corpse in the medicinal hotel?"
Clovis left and picked up one of the black cabs outside
Back to the mild west of London, feeling a kind of
Ecstasy he could not reflect on, so pure it was.

71

If the green man with the ribbony horse did exist
He had the gift of talking through his arse. Yes!
Reflection had begun: there is no battle between
'Spirit' and matter because matter will dominate always.
Thank God that minds can be so secondary given how
Absurd they can be — say Vaughan's and Penelope's.
Imagine perpetual flowering — like ice-cream and
Champagne for breakfast every day. Beauty is a gift
From matter, a brief thing that shines in consciousness.
Well, that won't do will it! Like many, Clovis was hooked
On the line *Death is the mother of beauty*, but was
Unconvinced by what Stevens seemed to mean by it. Let's say
Beauty is the opposite of death and decay
Like recto is the opposite of verso.

72

All that's a touch beside the point and a touch banal
And why the 'ecstasy'? Because for him acceptance
Of matter was coming home to a stern but fair father.
Not Stevens' 'mother' — father. But this was too final
For a man like Clovis. All of him yearned for a
Responding cry from — OK — *spirit*. He got it. It came
As he picked up a packet of the loose-leaf tea Susan
Would travel across London to buy. All of their life
Together compressed to seconds and the sight of her
As she would be now, dutiful at her desk printing off
Undergrad essays, birthday cards, the bed life with her,
The reality of her — matter against flim-flam.
He phoned her and said this. Shared love of Johnny Cash is why.
"Your name is Sue. How do you do. We're all gonna die."

THE END

www.ingramcontent.com/pod-product-compliance
Lightning Source LLC
Chambersburg PA
CBHW011957060426
42444CB00046B/3457